FIRST THOUSAND WORDS

IN RUSSIAN

With Internet-linked pronunciation guide

Heather Amery

Illustrated by Stephen Cartwright

Russian edition translated and typeset by AST-Press, Moscow

Edited by Mairi Mackinnon

Russian language consultants: Clare Mitchell and Marina Demidova

Reading the Russian alphabet

Russian is written in the Cyrillic (say *sirilick*) alphabet. This may look strange at first, but it is quite easy to learn. Once you have looked at the alphabet, try writing your name in the Cyrillic alphabet, and then some other names. This is a good way to learn the letters and their sounds.

There are many Russian words that are very similar to English, but are written in the Cyrillic alphabet and pronounced in the Russian way. For example, a mask is маска, "*maska*", and a lamp is лампа, "*lampa*". You will be surprised by the number of words you recognize.

If you look at the list below, you will see that some Cyrillic letters look like our alphabet, but some look very different. Watch out, because the ones that look the same may have a different sound: B, for example, sounds like *v* in van, P sounds like *r* in root and H sounds like *n* in net. So when you see ванна you say "*vanna*" (bath), when you see радио you say "*radeeo*" (radio) and when you see банан you say "*banan*" (banana).

Vowels

printed		written		
А	а	*A*	*a*	*a* as in *mat*
О	о	*O*	*o*	*aw* as in *paw*
Э	э	*э*	*э*	*e* as in *bed*
У	у	*У*	*у*	*oo* as in *boot*
Ы	ы	*Ы*	*ы*	*i* as in *rip* (tongue pushed back)
Я	я	*Я*	*я*	*ya* as in *yak*
Ё	ё	*Ё*	*ё*	*yaw* as in *yawn*
Е	е	*E*	*e*	*ye* as in *yet*
Ю	ю	*Ю*	*ю*	*yoo* as in *useful*
И	и	*И*	*и*	*ee* as in *meet*
Й	й	*Й*	*й*	*y* as in *boy*

Hard and soft vowels

Hard: а о э у ы
Soft: я ё е ю й

For each English vowel you will notice that there are two in Russian, a hard and a soft. The soft vowel has a "y" sound before it. To hear the difference, practise saying а я, "*a ya*".

Consonants

printed		written		
Б	б	*Б*	*б*	*b* as in *book*
В	в	*В*	*в*	*v* as in *van*
Г	г	*Г*	*г*	*g* as in *get*
Д	д	*D*	*g*	*d* as in *day*
Ж	ж	*Ж*	*ж*	*zh* like the *s* in *pleasure*
З	з	*З*	*з*	*z* as in *zoo*
К	к	*К*	*к*	*k* as in *kit*
Л	л	*Л*	*л*	*l* as in *table*, before a hard vowel, or *l* as in *leaf*, before a soft vowel
М	м	*М*	*м*	*m* as in *milk*
Н	н	*Н*	*н*	*n* as in *net*
П	п	*П*	*п*	*p* as in *pot*
Р	Р	*Р*	*р*	*r* as in *rock*
С	с	*С*	*с*	*s* as in *sit*
Т	т	*Т*	*m̄*	*t* as in *top*
Ф	ф	*Ф*	*ф*	*f* as in *fan*
Х	х	*Х*	*х*	*ch* as in Scottish *loch*
Ц	ц	*Ц*	*ц*	*ts* as in *cats*
Ч	ч	*Ч*	*ч*	*ch* as in *cheese*
Ш	ш	*Ш*	*ш*	*sh* as in *fresh*
Щ	щ	*Щ*	*щ*	*shch* as in *fresh cheese*
Ъ	ъ	*Ъ*	*ъ*	'hard sign' (very rare), gives the letter before it a 'hard' sound.
ь	ь	*ь*	*ь*	'soft sign', gives the letter before it a 'soft' sound.

On every big picture across two pages, there is a little yellow duck to look for. Can you find it?

Saying Russian words

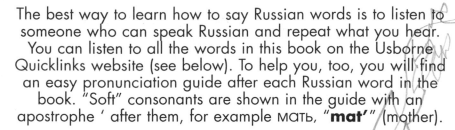

The best way to learn how to say Russian words is to listen to someone who can speak Russian and repeat what you hear. You can listen to all the words in this book on the Usborne Quicklinks website (see below). To help you, too, you will find an easy pronunciation guide after each Russian word in the book. "Soft" consonants are shown in the guide with an apostrophe ' after them, for example мать, "**mat'**" (mother).

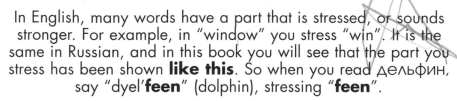

In English, many words have a part that is stressed, or sounds stronger. For example, in "window" you stress "win". It is the same in Russian, and in this book you will see that the part you stress has been shown **like this**. So when you read дельфин, say "dyel'**feen**" (dolphin), stressing "**feen**".

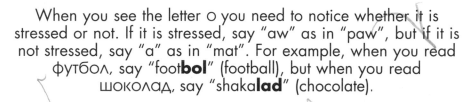

When you see the letter o you need to notice whether it is stressed or not. If it is stressed, say "aw" as in "paw", but if it is not stressed, say "a" as in "mat". For example, when you read футбол, say "foot**bol**" (football), but when you read шоколад, say "shaka**lad**" (chocolate).

Hear the words on the Internet

You can listen to all the words in this book, read by a native Russian speaker, on the Usborne Quicklinks Website. Just go to **www.usborne-quicklinks.com** and enter the keywords **1000 russian**. There you can:

- listen to the first thousand words in Russian
- find links to other useful websites about Russia and the Russian language.

Your computer needs a sound card (almost all computers have these) and may also need a small program, called an audio player, such as RealPlayer® or Windows® Media Player. These programs are free, and if you don't already have a copy, you can download one from the Usborne Quicklinks Website.

Note for parents and guardians

Please ensure that your children read and follow the Internet safety guidelines displayed on the Usborne Quicklinks Website.

The links in Usborne Quicklinks are regularly reviewed and updated. However, the content of a website may change at any time, and Usborne Publishing is not responsible for the content on any website other than its own. We recommend that children are supervised while on the Internet, that they do not use Internet chat rooms and that you use Internet filtering software to block unsuitable material. For more information, see the **Net Help** area on the Usborne Quicklinks Website.

Дома  doma

ванна
vanna

мыло
mila

кран
kran

туалетная бумага
tooa**lyet**-naya boo**ma**ga

зубная щётка
zoo**bna**ya **shchot**ka

вода
va**da**

унитаз
oonee**taz**

губка
goobka

раковина
rakaveena

душ
doosh

полотенце
pala**tyen**tse

кровать
kra**vat'**

ванная
vannaya

гостиная
ga**stee**naya

зубная паста
zoo**bna**ya **pas**ta

радио
radeeo

подушка
pa**doosh**ka

компакт-диск
kam**pakt deesk**

ковёр
ka**vyor**

софа
sa**fa**

4

СТУЛ
stool

пуховое одеяло
poo**ho**vaye adye**ya**la

расчёска
ras**chos**ka

простыня
prasti**nya**

коврик
kovreek

ШКАФ
shkaf

ПОДУШКА
pa**doosh**ka

СПАЛЬНЯ

spal'nya

КОМОД
ka**mod**

зеркало
zyerkala

щётка
shchotka

ЛАМПА
lampa

ХОЛЛ

holl

картины
kar**tee**ni

вешалка
vyeshalka

телефон
tele**fon**

батарея
bata**ryey**a

видеокассета
veedeokas**syet**a

газета
ga**zyet**a

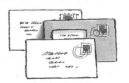

СТОЛ
stol

письма
pees'ma

лестница
lestneetsa

Кухня

koohnya

ХОЛОДИЛЬНИК
hala**deel'**neek

стаканы
sta**ka**ni

часы
cha**si**

табурет
taboo**ryet**

чайные ложки
chayniye **lozh**kee

выключатель
viklyoo-**cha**tyel'

стиральный порошок
stee**ral'**niy para**shok**

КЛЮЧ
klyooch

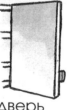

дверь
dver'

пылесос
pilye**sos**

кастрюли
ka**stryoo**lee

ВИЛКИ
veelkee

фартук
fartook

гладильная доска
gla**deel'**naya das**ka**

МУСОР
moosar

МОЙКА
moyka

 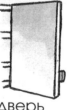

ЧАЙНИК
chayneek

НОЖИ
na**zhee**

ШВАБРА
shvabra

ТРЯПКА ДЛЯ ПЫЛИ
tryapka dlya **pi**lee

КАФЕЛЬ
kafyel'

ЩЁТКА
shchotka

СТИРАЛЬНАЯ МАШИНА
stee**ral'**naya ma**shee**na

СОВОК
sa**vok**

ЯЩИК
yashcheek

БЛЮДЦА
blyootsa

СКОВОРОДА
skavara**da**

ПЛИТА
plee**ta**

ЛОЖКИ
lozhkee

ТАРЕЛКИ
ta**ryel**kee

УТЮГ
oo**tyoog**

КЛАДОВКА
kla**dov**ka

КУХОННОЕ ПОЛОТЕНЦЕ
koohannaye pala**tyen**tse

ЧАШКИ
chashkee

СПИЧКИ
speechkee

ЩЁТКА
shchotka

МИСКИ
meeskee

тачка
tachka

улей
ooley

улитка
ooleetka

кирпичи
keerpeechee

Сад sad

лейка
leyka

голубь
goloob'

лопата
lapata

божья коровка
bozh'ya karovka

мусорный бак
moosarniy bak

семена
syemena

сарай
saray

червяк
chervyak

цветы
tsvyeti

поливальная установка
palee-val'naya oostanovka

мотыга
matiga

оса
asa

пчела
pchye**la**

СОВОК
sa**vok**

КОСТЬ
kost'

ЖИВАЯ ИЗГОРОДЬ
zhi**va**ya **eez**garad'

ВИЛЫ
veeli

ГАЗОНОКОСИЛКА
gazona-ka**seel**ka

ТРОПИНКА
tra**peen**ka

ЛИСТЬЯ
leest'ya

ДЕРЕВО
deryeva

ДЫМ
dim

ГУСЕНИЦА
goosyeneetsa

ГРАБЛИ
grablee

ГНЕЗДО
gnyez**do**

ВЕТКИ
vyetkee

ТЕПЛИЦА
tye**pleet**sa

ТРАВА
tra**va**

КОЛЯСКА
ka**lyas**ka

ЛЕСТНИЦА
lestneetsa

КОСТЁР
ka**styor**

ШЛАНГ
shlang

ТИСКИ
teeskee

наждачная бумага
nazhdachnaya
boomaga

дрель
dryel'

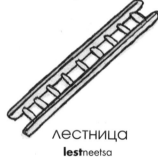

лестница
lestneetsa

ПИЛА
peela

ОПИЛКИ
apeelkee

календарь
kalyendar'

ящик для инструментов
yashcheek dlya eenstroo-myentav

Мастерская
mastyerskaya

шурупы
shooroopi

отвёртка
atvyortka

доска
daska

стружки
strooshkee

перочинный нож
pyeracheenniy nozh

КНОПКИ
knopkee

ПАУК
pa-**ook**

ВИНТЫ
veen**ti**

ГАЙКИ
gaykee

ПАУТИНА
pa-oo**tee**na

БОЧКА
bochka

МУХА
mooha

ТОПОР
ta**por**

РУЛЕТКА
roo**lyet**ka

МОЛОТОК
mala**tok**

НАПИЛЬНИК
na**peel'**neek

банка с краской
banka s**kras**koy

ДРОВА
dra**va**

ГВОЗДИ
gvozdee

ВЕРСТАК
vyer**stak**

БАНКИ
bankee

РУБАНОК
roo**ba**nak

11

Улица

*oo*leetsa

магазин

maga**zeen**

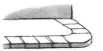

яма

yama

кафе

ka-**fe**

скорая помощь

skoraya **po**mashch'

тротуар

trato**oar**

антенна

an**ten**na

труба

troo**ba**

крыша

krisha

экскаватор

ekska**va**tar

гостиница

gas**tee**neetsa

автобус

av**to**boos

мужчина

moozh**chee**na

милицейская машина

meelee-**tsey**skaya ma**shee**na

трубы

troobi

отбойный молоток

at**boy**niy mala**tok**

школа

shkola

площадка для и

plash**chad**ka dlya **eeg**

12

такси
tak**see**

переход
pere**hod**

фабрика
fabreeka

грузовик
grooza**veek**

светофор
svyeta**for**

кинотеатр
keenate**atr**

фургон
foor**gon**

каток
ka**tok**

прицеп
pree**tsep**

дом
dom

рынок
rinak

лестница
lestneetsa

мотоцикл
mata**tseek**l

дом
dom

велосипед
velasee**pyed**

пожарная машина
pa**zhar**naya ma**shee**na

милиционер
meelee-tseea**nyer**

машина
ma**shee**na

женщина
zhenshcheena

уличный
фонарь
ooleechniy
fa**nar'**

13

железная дорога
zhe**lyez**naya
da**ro**ga

игральные кости
ee**gral'**niye
kostee

блок-флейта
blok-**fley**ta

робот
robat

барабаны
bara**ba**ni

ожерелье
azhe**ryel'**ye

фотоаппарат
fota-appa**rat**

бусы
boosi

куклы
kookli

гитара
gee**ta**ra

кольцо
kal'**tso**

кукольный дом
kookal'niy **dom**

Магазин игрушек
maga**zeen**
ee**groo**shek

губная гармошка
goo**bna**ya gar**mosh**ka

свисток
svee**stok**

кубики
koobeekee

замок
zamak

**подводная
лодка**
pad**vod**naya **lod**ka

труба
trooba

стрелы
stryeli

ЛУК look

парашют para**shoot**

яхта **yah**ta

грим **greem**

каток ka**tok**

маски **mas**kee

гоночная машина **go**nachnaya ma**shee**na

лошадь-качалка **lo**shad'-ka**chal**ka

копилка ka**peel**ka

шарики **sha**reekee

марионетки mareea-**nyet**kee

рояль ra**yal'**

космонавты kasma**naf**ti

подъёмный кран pa**dyom**niy **kran**

пластилин plastee**leen**

ружьё roozh'**yo**

солдатики sal**da**teekee

краски **kras**kee

ракета ra**kye**ta

15

качели
ka**chyel**ee

песочница
pe**soch**neetsa

пикник
peek**neek**

воздушный
змей
vaz**doosh**niy
z**myey**

мороженое
ma**ro**zhenaye

собака
sa**ba**ka

калитка
ka**leet**ka

тропинка
tra**peen**ka

лягушка
lya**goosh**ka

горка для катания
gorka dlya ka**ta**neeya

Парк _{park}

скамейка
ska**myey**ka

головастики
gala**vas**teekee

озеро
ozyera

ролики
roleekee

куст
koost

малыш
ma**lish**

скейтборд
skeytbord

земля
zyem**lya**

прогулочная коляска
pra**goo**-lachnaya ka**lyas**ka

качели
ka**chyel**ee

дети
dyetee

трёхколёсный велосипед
tryohkal-**yos**niy vyela-see**pyed**

птицы
pteetsi

забор
za**bor**

мяч
myach

яхта
yahta

бечёвка
bye**chov**ka

лужа
loozha

утята
ooty**ata**

скакалка
ska**kal**ka

деревья
dye**ryev'**ya

клумба
kloomba

лебеди
lyebedee

поводок
pava**dok**

утки
ootkee

Зоопарк

zaa**park**

крыло
kri**lo**

орёл
ar**yol**

бегемот
bege**mot**

панда
panda

летучая мышь
lye**too**chaya **mish'**

горилла
ga**reel**la

кенгуру
kengoo**roo**

обезьяна
abyez**'ya**na

лапы
lapi

айсберг
aysbyerg

хвост
hvost

волк
volk

перья
pyer'ya

крокодил
kraka**deel**

пингвин
peen**gveen**

медведь
myed**vyed'**

пеликан
pelee**kan**

страус
straoos

дельфин
dyel'**feen**

жираф
zhi**raf**

лев
lyev

львята
l'**vya**ta

рога
ra**ga**

олень
a**len'**

вербглюд
vyer**blyood**

тюлень
tyoo**len'**

белый медведь
byeliy myed**vyed'**

черепаха
chere**pa**ha

хобот
hobat

носорог
nasa**rog**

бизон
bee**zon**

слон
slon

бобр
bobr

коза
ka**za**

зебра
zyebra

змея
zme**ya**

акула
a**koo**la

кит
keet

тигр
teegr

леопард
lyea**pard**

19

Путешествие

железная дорога
zhe**lyez**naya da**ro**ga

локомотив
lakama**teev**

буфера
boofye**ra**

вагоны
va**go**ni

машинист
mashee**neest**

товарный поезд
ta**var**niy **po**yest

платформа
plat**for**ma

контролёр
kantra**lyor**

чемодан
chema**dan**

касса-автомат
kassa-avta**mat**

вертолёт
vyerta**lyot**

Вокзал vak**zal**

Гараж ga**razh**

семафор
sema**for**

рюкзак
ryook**zak**

фары
fari

двигатель
dveegatyel'

колесо
kalye**so**

аккумулятор
akoomoo-**lya**tar

20

самолёт
samalyot

стюардесса
styooardessa

взлётная полоса
vslyotnaya palasa

диспетчерская вышка
deespyetcherskaya vishka

Аэропорт
a-eraport

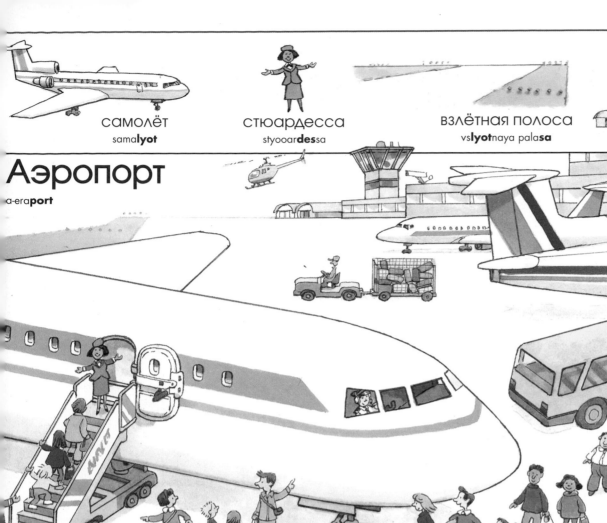

стюард
styooard

пилот
peelot

автомойка
aftamoyka

багажник
bagazhneek

бензин
byenzeen

аварийная машина
avareenaya masheena

АВТОМОЙКА

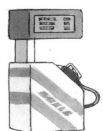

бензоколонка
byenzakalonka

бензовоз
byenzavoz

гаечный ключ
gayechniy klyooch

шина
sheena

капот
kapot

масло
masla

ветряная мельница
vyetrya-naya **myel'**neetsa

воздушный шар
vaz**doosh**niy **shar**

бабочка
babachka

ящерица
yashchereetsa

камни
kamnee

лиса
lee**sa**

ручей
roo**chey**

дорожный
указатель
da**rozh**niy
ooka**za**tyel'

ёж
yozh

шлюз
shlyooz

Сельская местность

syel'skaya
myestnast'

гора
ga**ra**

белка
byelka

лес
lyes

барсук
bar**sook**

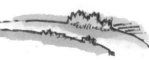

река
rye**ka**

дорога
da**ro**ga

палатки
pa**lat**kee

канал
ka**nal**

брёвна
bryovna

деревня
de**ryev**nya

мотылёк
mati**lyok**

МОСТ
most

баржа
barzha

ВОДОПАД
vada**pad**

сова
sa**va**

туннель
too**nel'**

лисята
lee**sya**ta

крот
krot

рыбак
ri**bak**

КАМНИ
kamnee

жаба
zhaba

поезд
poyest

автофургон
aftafoor**gon**

ХОЛМ
holm

23

СТОГ
stok

КОЛЛИ
kollee

УТКИ
ootkee

ЯГНЯТА
yag**nya**ta

ПРУД
prood

ЦЫПЛЯТА
tsi**plya**ta

ЧЕРДАК
cher**dak**

СВИНАРНИК
svee**nar**neek

БЫК
bik

УТЯТА
ooty**a**ta

КУРЯТНИК
koo**ryat**neek

ТРАКТОР
traktar

Ферма

fyerma

ПЕТУХ
pye**tooh**

ГУСИ
goosee

ЦИСТЕРНА
tsees**ter**na

АМБАР
am**bar**

ЗЕМЛЯ
zyem**lya**

ТЕЛЕЖКА
tye**lyesh**ka

фермер
fyermyer

поле
polye

куры
koori

телёнок
tyelyonak

забор
zabor

седло
syedlo

коровник
karovneek

корова
karova

плуг
ploog

сад
sad

конюшня
kanyooshnya

поросята
parasyata

пастушка
pastooshka

индюки
eendyookee

пугало
poogala

дом на ферме
dom na fyermye

сено
syena

овцы
ovtsi

брикеты соломы
breekyeti salomi

лошадь
loshad'

свиньи
sveen'ee

У моря

oo **mo**rya

парусник
paroosneek

море
morye

весло
vyes**lo**

маяк
ma**yak**

лопата
la**pa**ta

ведро
vye**dro**

морская звезда
mar**ska**ya zvyez**da**

замок из песка
zamak eez pyes**ka**

зонтик
zonteek

флаг
flag

раковина
rakaveena

моряк
ma**ryak**

краб
krab

чайка
chayka

остров
ostrav

моторка
ma**tor**ka

водный лыжни
vodniy **lizh**neek

ВОЛНЫ
volni

ШЛЯПА
shlyapa

УТЁС
oo**tyos**

КОРАБЛЬ
ka**rabl'**

БАЙДАРКА
bay**dar**ka

КАНАТ
ka**nat**

ГАЛЬКА
gal'ka

ВОДОРОСЛИ
vodaraslee

СЕТЬ
syet'

ВЕСЛО
vyes**lo**

РЫБАЧЬЯ ЛОДКА
ri**bach'**ya **lod**ka

ЛАСТЫ
lasti

ОСЛИК
osleek

РЫБА
riba

ШЕЗЛОНГ
shez**long**

КУПАЛЬНИК
koo**pal'**neek

ТАНКЕР
tankyer

ПЛЯЖ
plyazh

ВЁСЕЛЬНАЯ ЛОДКА
vyosel'naya **lod**ka

27

НОЖНИЦЫ
nozhneetsi

$$2 + 2 = 4$$
$$3 + 2 = 5$$

примеры
pree**myer**i

резинка
rye**zeen**ka

линейка
lee**nyey**ka

фотографии
fata**gra**fee

фломастеры
fla**mas**teri

КНОПКИ
knopkee

краски
kraskee

мальчик
mal'cheek

карандаш
karan**dash**

В ШКОЛЕ
v**shkol**ye

ДОСКА
da**ska**

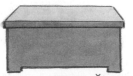

письменный стол
pees'myenniy **stol**

КНИГИ
kneegee

ручка
roochka

КЛЕЙ
kley

мел
myel

рисунок
ree**soo**nak

сорное ведро
oosarnaye vye**dro**

учительница
oo**chee**tel'neetsa

коробка
ka**rop**ka

карта
karta

кисточка
keestochka

потолок
pata**lok**

стена
stye**na**

пол
pol

тетрадь
tyet**rad'**

абвгдеёжз
ийклмнопр
стуфхцчш
щъыьэюя

алфавит
alfa**veet**

значок
zna**chok**

аквариум
ak**va**reeoom

бумага
boo**ma**ga

жалюзи
zhalyoozee

мольберт
mal'**byert**

абвгдеёжз
ийклмнопр
стуфхцчш
щъыьэюя

ерная ручка
yer**na**ya **rooch**ka

растение
ra**styen**eeye

глобус
globoos

девочка
dyevachka

карандаши
karanda**shee**

**настольная
лампа**
na**stol'**naya **lam**pa

мольберт
mal'**byert**

29

медбрат
myed**brat**

вата
vata

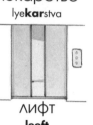

лекарство
lye**kar**stva

лифт
leeft

халат
ha**lat**

костыли
kasti**lee**

таблетки
ta**blyet**kee

поднос
pad**nos**

часы
cha**si**

термометр
tyer**mo**metr

занавеска
zana-**vyes**ka

Больница

bal'**neet**sa

плюшевый мишка
plyoosheviy **meesh**ka

яблоко
yablaka

гипс
geeps

бинт
beent

кресло-каталка
kryesla-ka**tal**ka

картинка-
конструктор
kar**teen**ka-kan**strook**tar

врач
vrach

шприц
shpreets

30

Врач

vrach

шлёпанцы
shlyopantsi

компьютер
kamp'**yoo**ter

пластырь
plastir'

банан
ba**nan**

виноград
veena**grad**

корзина
kar**zee**na

игрушки
ee**groosh**kee

груша
groosha

открытки
at**krit**kee

подгузник
pad**goos**neek

палка
palka

телевизор
tele**vee**zar

ночная рубашка
nach**na**ya roo**bash**ka

пижама
pee**zha**ma

апельсин
apel'**seen**

салфетки
sal**fyet**kee

комиксы
komeeksi

приёмная
pree**yom**naya

Вечеринка

vyeche**reen**ka

ПОДАРКИ
pa**dar**kee

воздушный
шарик

vaz**doosh**niy
shareek

ШОКОЛАД
shaka**lad**

конфета
kan**fye**ta

ОКНО
ak**no**

фейерверк
feyer**vyerk**

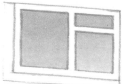

лента
lyenta

ПОДАРКИ
pa**dar**kee

торт
tort

СОЛОМИНКА
sa**lo**meenka

свеча
svye**cha**

гирлянда
geer**lyan**da

игрушки
ee**groosh**kee

мандарин
manda**reen**

САЛЯМИ
sa**lya**mee

кассета
kas**syet**a

сосиска
sa**sees**ka

ЧИПСЫ
cheepsi

МАСКАРАДНЫЕ КОСТЮМЫ
maska-**rad**niye
kas**tyoo**mi

ВИШНЯ
veeshnya

ФРУКТОВЫЙ СОК
frook**to**viy **sok**

МАЛИНА
ma**lee**na

КЛУБНИКА
kloob**nee**ka

ЛАМПОЧКА
lampachka

бутерброд
bootyer**brod**

масло
masla

печенье
pye**chen'**ye

сыр
seer

хлеб
hlyeb

скатерть
skatyert'

33

грейпфрут
greyp**froot**

морковь
mar**kov'**

цветная капуста
tsvyet**na**ya ka**poos**ta

лук-порей
look-pa**rey**

гриб
greeb

огурец
agoo**ryets**

лимон
lee**mon**

сельдерей
syel'de**rey**

абрикос
abree**kos**

дыня
dinya

Магазин

maga**zeen**

пакет
pa**kyet**

сыр

овощи и фрукты

лук
look

капуста
ka**poos**ta

персик
pyerseek

салат
sa**lat**

горох
ga**roh**

помидор
pamee**dor**

ЯЙЦА
yaytsa

СЛИВА
sleeva

МУКА
moo**ka**

ВЕСЫ
vye**si**

БАНКИ
bankee

МЯСО
myasa

АНАНАС
ana**nas**

ЙОГУРТ
yogoort

КОРЗИНА
kar**zee**na

БУТЫЛКИ
boo**til**kee

СУМОЧКА
soomachka

КОШЕЛЁК
kashe**lyok**

ДЕНЬГИ
dyen'gee

КОНСЕРВЫ
kan**syer**vi

КАРТОФЕЛЬ
kar**to**fel'

ШПИНАТ
shpee**nat**

БОБЫ
ba**bi**

КАССА
kassa

ТЫКВА
tikva

ТЕЛЕЖКА
tye**lyesh**ka

Еда _{yeda}

завтрак
zavtrak

обед
a**byed**

варёное яйцо
va**ryon**aye yay**tso**

тосты
tosti

джем
djem

кофе
kofye

яичница
ya**eech**neetsa

СЛИВКИ
sleevkee

МОЛОКО
mala**ko**

ХЛОПЬЯ
hlop'ya

какао
ka**ka**o

сахар
sahar

мёд
myod

СОЛЬ
sol'

перец
pyeryets

чай
chay

чайник
chayneek

блины
bleeni

булочки
boolachkee

36

ужин
oozheen

ветчина
vyetchee**na**

суп
soop

омлет
am**lyet**

палочки
palachkee

салат
sa**lat**

гамбургер
gamboorgyer

цыплёнок
tsi**plyo**nak

рис
rees

соус
so-oos

спагетти
spa**get**tee

картофельное пюре
kar**to**fel'naye pyoo**re**

пицца
peetsa

чипсы
cheepsi

пудинг
poodeeng

Я ya

ГОЛОВА
ga**la**va

ВОЛОСЫ
volasi

ЛИЦО
lee**tso**

рука
roo**ka**

ЛОКОТЬ
lokat'

ЖИВОТ
zhi**vot**

ПАЛЬЦЫ НОГИ
pal'tsi na**gee**

СТУПНЯ
stoop**nya**

НОГА
na**ga**

КОЛЕНО
ka**lyen**a

бровь
brov'

глаз
glaz

нос
nos

щека
shche**ka**

рот
rot

губы
goobi

зубы
zoobi

язык
ya**zik**

подбородок
padba**ro**dak

уши
ooshee

шея
sheya

плечи
plyechee

грудь
grood'

спина
spee**na**

ЯГОДИЦЫ
yaga**deet**si

кисть руки
keest' roo**kee**

большой палец
bal'**shoy pa**lyets

пальцы
pal'tsi

Моя одежда

maya adyezhda

носки
naskee

трусы
troosee

майка
mayka

брюки
bryookee

джинсы
djeensi

футболка
footbolka

юбка
yoopka

рубашка
roobashka

галстук
galstook

шорты
shorti

колготки
kalgotkee

платье
plat'ye

джемпер
djempyer

свитер
sveeter

кофта
kofta

шарф
sharf

носовой платок
nasavoy platok

кроссовки
krassovkee

ботинки
bateenkee

сандалии
sandalee

сапоги
sapagee

перчатки
pyerchatkee

ремень
ryemen'

пряжка
pryashka

молния
molneeya

шнурок
shnoorok

пуговицы
poogaveetsi

петли
pyetlee

карманы
karmani

пальто
pal'to

куртка
koortka

кепка
kyepka

шляпа
shlyapa

Люди  **lyoo**dee

повар

povar

актёр

ak**tyor**

актриса

ak**tree**sa

танцоры

tan**tsor**i

певцы

pyev**tsi**

космонавт

kazma**naft**

мясник

myas**neek**

милиционер

meelee-tseea**nyer**

женщина-
милиционер

zhenshcheena-
meelee-tseea**nyer**

плотник

plotneek

пожарник

pa**zhar**neek

художник

hoo**dozh**neek

судья

sood'**ya**

механики

mye**ha**neekee

40

парикмахер
pareek-**ma**hyer

водитель грузовика
va**dee**tyel' groozavee**ka**

водитель автобуса
va**dee**tyel' av**to**boosa

официант
afee-tsee**ant**

официантка
afee-tsee**ant**ka

почтальон
pachtal'**on**

зубной врач
zoob**noy vrach**

водолаз
vada**laz**

маляр
ma**lyar**

пекарь
pyekar'

Семья

syem'**ya**

тётя
tyotya

дядя
dyadya

двоюродный
брат
dva**yoo**radniy **brat**

сын
sin

дочь
doch'

мать
mat'

отец
a**tyets**

дедушка
dyedooshka

бабушка
babooshka

брат
brat

сестра
syes**tra**

жена
zhe**na**

муж
moozh

Занятия

zanyateeya

смеяться
smeyat'sa

улыбаться
oolibat'sa

плакать
plakat'

думать
doomat'

слушать
slooshat'

ловить
laveet'

бросать
brasat'

ломать
lamat'

рисовать
reesavat'

писать
peesat'

рубить
roobeet'

резать
ryezat'

есть
yest'

разговаривать
razga-vareevat'

копать
kapat'

нести
nyestee

пить
peet'

делать
dyelat'

прыгать
prigat'

ползти
palstee

танцевать
tantsevat'

мыть
mit'

вязать
vyazat'

42

играть
ee**grat'**

смотреть
sma**tryet'**

залезать
zalye**zat'**

драться
drat'sa

спать
spat'

брать
brat'

прыгать
prigat'

шить
sheet'

ждать
zhdat'

готовить еду
ga**to**veet' ye**doo**

прятаться
pryatat'sa

читать
chee**tat'**

покупать
pakoo**pat'**

толкать
tal**kat'**

подметать
padmye**tat'**

петь
pyet'

собирать
sabee**rat'**

дуть
doot'

тянуть
tya**noot'**

падать
padat'

идти
eed**tee**

бежать
bye**zhat'**

сидеть
see**dyet'**

43

Антонимы

antoneemi

далеко
dalyeko

близко
bleezka

хороший
haroshee

плохой
plahoy

верхний
vyerhnee

нижний
neezhnee

холодный
halodniy

горячий
garyachee

мокрый
mokriy

сухой
soohoy

над
nad

под
pod

грязный
gryazniy

чистый
cheestiy

толстый
tolstiy

тонкий
tonkee

открытый
atkritiy

закрытый
zakritiy

маленький
malyen'kee

большой
bal'shoy

мало
mala

много
mnoga

первый
pyerviy

последний
paslyednee

левый
lyeviy

44

снаружи
snaroozhee

внутри
vnootree

легко
lyehko

трудно
troodna

пустой
poostoy

полный
polniy

мягкий
myahkee

твёрдый
tvyordiy

спереди
speryedee

высоко
visako

медленно
myedlyenna

быстро
bistra

сзади
szadee

низко
neezka

длинный
dleenniy

короткий
karotkee

мёртвый
myortviy

живой
zhivoy

темно
tyemno

светло
svyetlo

старый
stariy

наверху
navyerhoo

правый
praviy

новый
noviy

внизу
vneezoo

45

ДНИ dnee

понедельник
panye**dyel'**neek

вторник
v**tor**neek

среда
srye**da**

четверг
chet**vyerg**

пятница
pyatneetsa

суббота
soob**bo**ta

воскресенье
vaskre-**syen'**ye

календарь
kalyen**dar'**

утро
ootra

вечер
vyecher

солнце
solntse

ночь
noch'

луна
loo**na**

звезда
zvyez**da**

космос
kosmas

планета
pla**nyet**a

ракета
ra**kyet**a

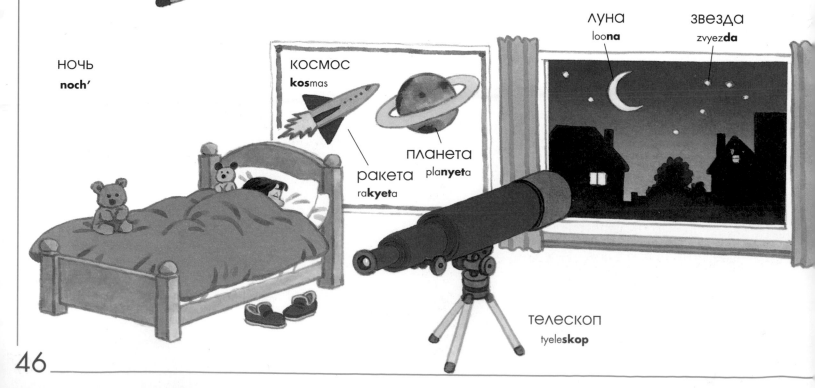

телескоп
tyele**skop**

Праздники

prazneekee

день рождения
dyen' zh**dyen**eeya

подарок
pa**da**rak

свеча
svye**cha**

праздничный торт
prazneechniy **tort**

поздравительная открытка
pazdra-**vee**tel'naya at**krit**ka

отпуск
otpoosk

свадьба
svad'ba

подружка невесты
pa**droosh**ka nye**vyes**ti

невеста и жених
nye**vyes**ta ee zhe**neeh**

фотоаппарат
fota-appa**rat**

фотограф
fa**to**graf

Рождество
razhdest**vo**

северный олень
syeverniy a**len'**

сани
sanee

ёлка
yolka

Дед Мороз
dyed ma**roz**

Погода
pa**go**da

ЗОНТИК
zonteek

ДОЖДЬ
doshd'

МОЛНИЯ
molneeya

ветер
vyetyer

ТУМАН
too**man**

ТУМАН
too**man**

СОЛНЦЕ
solntse

ОБЛАКА
oblaka

небо
nyeba

СНЕГ
snyeg

роса
ra**sa**

мороз
ma**roz**

радуга
radooga

Времена года
vremye**na go**da

весна
vyes**na**

лето
lyeta

осень
osyen'

зима
zee**ma**

Домашние животные

damashneeye zhivotniye

хомяк
hamyak

ветврач
vyetvrach

будка
bootka

морская свинка
marskaya sveenka

собака
sabaka

волнистый попугайчик
valneestiy papoo-gaycheek

щенок
shchenok

попугай
papoogay

корм
korm

клюв
klyoof

канарейка
kanaryeyka

кролик
kroleek

клетка
klyetka

кошка
koshka

корзина
karzeena

котёнок
katyonak

молоко
malako

мышь
mish'

золотая рыбка
zalataya ribka

Спорт и физкультура

sport ee
feeskool'-**too**ra

баскетбол
baskyet**bol**

гребля
gryeblya

парусный спорт
paroosniy **sport**

виндсёрфинг
veend**syor**feeng

сноубординг
sno-oo**bor**deeng

ракетка
ra**kyet**ka

теннис
tennees

американский
футбол
ameree**kan**skee
foot**bol**

гимнастика
geem**nas**teeka

крикет
kreekyet

каратэ
kara**te**

бита
beeta

мяч
m**yach**

танцы
tantsi

бейсбол
beys**bol**

удочка
oodachka

наживка
na**zhiv**ka

рыбалка
ri**bal**ka

регби
regbee

прыжки в воду
prish**kee vvo**doo

бассейн
bas**seyn**

плавание
plavaneeye

бег
byeg

стрельба из лука
stryel'**ba** eez **loo**ka

мишень
mee**shyen'**

дельтапланеризм
dyel'ta-planye**reezm**

бег трусцой
byeg troos**tsoy**

шлем
shlyem

велоспорт
vyela**sport**

альпинизм
al'pee**neezm**

дзюдо
dzyoo**do**

лошадь
loshad'

пони
ponee

шкафчик
shkafcheek

футбол
foot**bol**

верховая езда
vyerha**va**ya yez**da**

раздевалка
razdye-**val**ka

бадминтон
badmeen**ton**

настольный тенис
na**stol'**niy **ten**nees

коньки
kan'**kee**

фигурное катание
fee**goor**naye ka**ta**neeye

лыжная палка
lizhnaya **pal**ka

подъёмник
pa**dyom**neek

лыжи
lizhee

горные лыжи
gorniye **li**zhee

борьба сумо
bar'**ba soo**mo

51

Цвета

tsvyeta

оранжевый
aranjeviy

зелёный
zyelyoniy

чёрный
chorniy

серый
syeriy

красный
krasniy

коричневый
kareechnyeviy

розовый
rozaviy

белый
byeliy

синий
seenee

пурпурный
poorpoorniy

жёлтый
zholtiy

Фигуры

feegoori

ромб
romb

конус
konoos

прямоугольник
pryama-oogol'neek

круг
kroog

звезда
zvyezda

куб
koob

овал
aval

треугольник
trye-oogol'neek

квадрат
kvadrat

полумесяц
paloo-myesyats

Числа

cheesla

1	ОДИН a**deen**	
2	ДВА **dva**	
3	ТРИ **tree**	
4	четыре che**tir**ye	
5	ПЯТЬ **pyat'**	
6	ШЕСТЬ **shest'**	
7	семь **syem'**	
8	ВОСЕМЬ **vos**yem'	
9	девять **dyev**yat'	
10	десять **dyes**yat'	
11	ОДИННАДЦАТЬ a**deen**natsat'	
12	двенадцать dvye**nat**sat'	
13	ТРИНАДЦАТЬ tree**nat**sat'	
14	четырнадцать che**tir**-natsat'	
15	ПЯТНАДЦАТЬ pyat**nat**sat'	
16	шестнадцать shest**nat**sat'	
17	семнадцать syem**nat**sat'	
18	ВОСЕМНАДЦАТЬ vasyem-**nat**sat'	
19	девятнадцать dyevyat**nat**sat'	
20	ДВАДЦАТЬ **dva**tsat'	

Луна-парк

loona-**park**

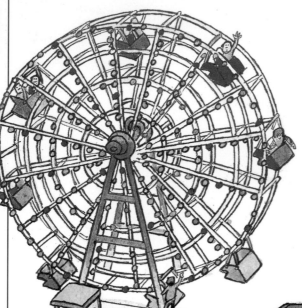

колесо обозрения

kalye**so** aba-**zryen**eeya

карусель

karoo**syel'**

мат

mat

американские горки

ameree-**kan**skeeye **gor**kee

набрось-кольцо

na**bros'**-kal'**tso**

поезд с привидениями

poyest spreevee-**dyen**eeyamee

попкорн

pap**korn**

американские горки

ameree-**kan**skeeye **gor**kee

тир

teer

электромобили

elektra-ma**bee**lee

сахарная вата

saharnaya **va**ta

Цирк

tseerk

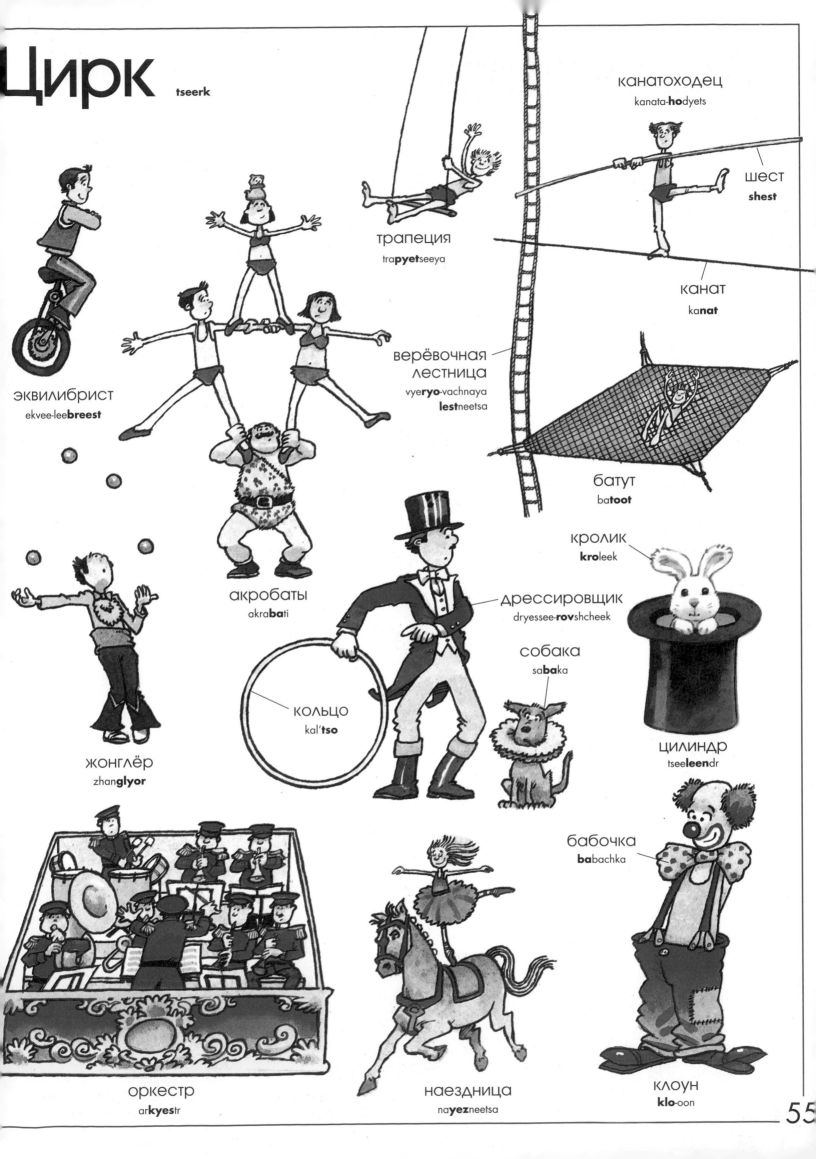

канатоходец
kanata-**ho**dyets

шест
shest

трапеция
tra**pyet**seeya

канат
ka**nat**

верёвочная
лестница
vye**ryo**-vachnaya
lestneetsa

эквилибрист
ekvee-lee**breest**

батут
ba**toot**

акробаты
akra**ba**ti

кролик
kroleek

дрессировщик
dryessee-**rov**shcheek

собака
sa**ba**ka

жонглёр
zhan**glyor**

кольцо
kal'**tso**

цилиндр
tsee**leen**dr

бабочка
babachka

оркестр
ar**kyes**tr

наездница
na**yez**neetsa

клоун
klo-oon

55

Word list

Here are all the Russian words in the book, in Cyrillic alphabetical order. To help you find words in the list, the Cyrillic alphabet is given below. Next to each word you can see how to pronounce it, in letters *like this*, and then its meaning in English.

а б в г д е ё ж з и й к л м н о п р с т у ф х ц ч ш щ ъ ы ь э ю я

а

абрикос, 34	*abree**kos***	apricot
аварийная машина, 21	*ava**ree**naya ma**shee**na*	breakdown lorry
автобус, 12	*av**to**boos*	bus
автомойка, 21	*afta**moy**ka*	car wash
автофургон, 23	*aftafoor**gon***	caravan
айсберг, 18	***ays**byerg*	iceberg
аквариум, 29	*ak**va**reeoom*	aquarium
аккумулятор, 20	*akoomoo-**lya**tar*	battery
акробаты, 55	*akra**ba**ti*	acrobats
актёр, 40	*ak**tyor***	actor
актриса, 40	*ak**tree**sa*	actress
акула, 19	*a**koo**la*	shark
алфавит, 29	*alfa**veet***	alphabet
альпинизм, 51	*al'pee**neezm***	climbing
амбар, 24	*am**bar***	barn
американские горки, 54	*ameree-**kan**skeeye **gor**kee*	helter-skelter, rollercoaster
американский футбол, 50	*ameree**kan**skee foot**bol***	American football
ананас, 35	*ana**nas***	pineapple
антенна, 12	*an**ten**na*	aerial
антонимы, 44	*an**to**neemi*	opposites
апельсин, 31	*apel'**seen***	orange (fruit)
аэропорт, 21	*a-era**port***	airport

б

бабочка, 22	***ba**bachka*	butterfly
бабочка, 55	***ba**bachka*	bow tie
бабушка, 41	***ba**booshka*	grandmother
багажник, 21	*ba**gazh**neek*	(car) boot
бадминтон, 51	*badmeen**ton***	badminton
байдарка, 27	*bay**dar**ka*	canoe
банан, 31	*ba**nan***	banana
банка с краской, 11	***ban**ka s**kras**koy*	paint pot
банки, 11, 35	***ban**kee*	jars
барабаны, 14	*bara**ba**ni*	drums
баржа, 23	***bar**zha*	barge
барсук, 22	*bar**sook***	badger
баскетбол, 50	*baskyet**bol***	basketball
бассейн, 50	*bas**seyn***	swimming pool
батарея, 5	*bata**ryey**a*	radiator
батут, 55	*ba**toot***	safety net
бег, 50	***byeg***	race
бег трусцой, 51	***byeg** troos**tsoy***	jogging
бегемот, 18	*bege**mot***	hippopotamus
бежать, 43	*bye**zhat'***	to run
бейсбол, 50	*beys**bol***	baseball
белка, 22	***byel**ka*	squirrel
белый, 52	***byel**iy*	white
белый медведь, 19	***byel**iy myed**vyed'***	polar bear
бензин, 21	*byen**zeen***	petrol
бензовоз, 21	*byenza**voz***	petrol tanker
бензоколонка, 21	*byenzaka**lon**ka*	petrol pump
бечёвка, 17	*bye**chov**ka*	string
бизон, 19	*bee**zon***	bison
бинт, 30	***beent***	bandage
бита, 50	***bee**ta*	bat (sports)
близко, 44	***bleez**ka*	near
блины, 36	*blee**ni***	pancakes

блок-флейта, 14	*blok-**flay**ta*	recorder
блюдца, 7	***blyoot**sa*	saucers
бобр, 19	***bo**br*	beaver
бобы, 35	*ba**bi***	beans
божья коровка, 8	***bozh'**ya ka**rov**ka*	ladybird
больница, 30	*bal'**neet**sa*	hospital
большой, 44	*bal'**shoy***	big
большой палец, 38	*bal'**shoy** **pa**lyets*	thumb
борьба сумо, 51	*bar'**ba soo**mo*	sumo wrestling
ботинки, 39	*ba**teen**kee*	shoes
бочка, 11	***boch**ka*	barrel
брат, 41	***brat***	brother
брать, 43	***brat'***	to take
брёвна, 23	***bryov**na*	logs
брикеты соломы, 25	*bree**kyet**i sa**lo**mi*	straw bales
бровь, 38	***brov'***	eyebrow
бросать, 42	*bra**sat'***	to throw
брюки, 39	*bry**oo**kee*	trousers
будка, 49	***boot**ka*	kennel
булочки, 36	***boo**lachkee*	bread rolls
бумага, 29	*boo**ma**ga*	paper
бусы, 14	***boo**si*	beads
бутерброд, 33	*bootyer**brod***	sandwich
бутылки, 35	*boo**til**kee*	bottles
буфера, 20	*boo**fye**ra*	buffers
бык, 24	***bik***	bull
быстро, 45	***bis**tra*	fast

в

в школе, 28	*v**shkol**ye*	at school
вагоны, 20	*va**go**ni*	carriages
ванна, 4	***van**na*	bath
ванная, 4	***van**naya*	bathroom
варёное яйцо, 36	*va**ryon**aye yay**tso***	boiled egg
вата, 30	***va**ta*	cotton wool
ведро, 26	*vye**dro***	bucket
велосипед, 13	*velasee**pyed***	bicycle
велоспорт, 51	*vyela**sport***	cycling
верблюд, 19	*vyer**blyood***	camel
верёвочная лестница, 55	*vye**ryo**-vachnaya **lest**neetsa*	rope ladder
верстак, 11	*vyer**stak***	workbench
вертолёт, 20	*vyerta**lyot***	helicopter
верхний, 44	***vyerh**nee*	top
верховая езда, 51	*vyerha**va**ya yez**da***	riding
весло, 26	*vyes**lo***	oar
весло, 27	*vyes**lo***	paddle
весна, 48	*vyes**na***	spring
весы, 35	*vye**si***	scales
ветврач, 49	*vyet**vrach***	vet
ветер, 48	***vyet**yer*	wind
ветки, 9	***vyet**kee*	sticks
ветряная мельница, 22	*vyetrya-**na**ya **myel'**neetsa*	windmill
ветчина, 37	*vyetchee**na***	ham
вечер, 46	***vyech**er*	evening
вечеринка, 32	*vyeche**reen**ka*	party
вешалка, 5	***vye**shalka*	pegs
вёсельная лодка, 27	***vyo**sel'naya **lod**ka*	rowing boat
взлётная полоса, 21	*vs**lyot**naya pala**sa***	runway
видеокассета, 5	*veedeokas**sye**ta*	video

вилки, 6	**veel**kee	forks
вилы, 9	**vee**li	(garden) fork
виндсёрфинг, 50	veend**syor**feeng	windsurfing
виноград, 31	veena**grad**	grapes
винты, 11	veen**ti**	bolts
вишня, 33	**veesh**nya	cherry
внизу, 45	vnee**zoo**	downstairs
внутри, 45	vnoo**tree**	in
вода, 4	va**da**	water
водитель автобуса, 41	va**dee**tyel' av**to**boosa	bus driver
водитель грузовика, 41	va**dee**tyel' groozavee**ka**	lorry driver
водный лыжник, 26	**vod**niy **lizh**neek	water-skier
водолаз, 41	vada**laz**	frogman
водопад, 23	vada**pad**	waterfall
водоросли, 27	**vo**daraslee	seaweed
воздушный змей, 16	vaz**doosh**niy z**myey**	kite
воздушный шар, 22	vaz**doosh**niy **shar**	hot-air balloon
воздушный шарик, 32	vaz**doosh**niy **sha**reek	balloon
вокзал, 20	vak**zal**	railway station
волк, 18	**volk**	wolf
волнистый попугайчик, 49	val**nees**tiy papoo**gay**cheek	budgerigar
волны, 27	**vol**ni	waves
волосы, 38	**vo**lasi	hair
восемнадцать, 53	vasyem-**nat**sat'	eighteen
восемь, 53	**vos**yem'	eight
воскресенье, 46	vaskre-**syen'**ye	Sunday
врач, 30, 31	**vrach**	doctor
времена года, 48	vremye**na go**da	seasons
вторник, 46	v**tor**neek	Tuesday
выключатель, 6	viklyoo-**cha**tyel'	switch
высоко, 45	visa**ko**	high
вязать, 42	vya**zat'**	to knit

Г

гаечный ключ, 21	**ga**yechniy **klyooch**	spanner
газета, 5	ga**zyet**a	newspaper
газонокосилка, 9	gazona-ka**seel**ka	lawnmower
гайки, 11	**gay**kee	nuts
галстук, 39	**gal**stook	tie
галька, 27	**gal'**ka	pebbles
гамбургер, 37	**gam**boorgyer	hamburger
гараж, 20	ga**razh**	garage
гвозди, 11	**gvoz**dee	nails
гимнастика, 50	geem**nas**teeka	gymnastics
гипс, 30	**geeps**	plaster cast
гирлянда, 32	geer**lyan**da	paper chain
гитара, 14	gee**ta**ra	guitar
гладильная доска, 6	gla**deel'**naya das**ka**	ironing board
глаз, 38	**glaz**	eye
глобус, 29	**glo**boos	globe
гнездо, 9	gnyez**do**	bird's nest
голова, 38	gala**va**	head
головастики, 16	gala**vas**teekee	tadpoles
голубь, 8	**go**loob'	pigeon
гоночная машина, 15	**go**nachnaya ma**shee**na	racing car
гора, 22	ga**ra**	mountain
горилла, 18	ga**reel**la	gorilla
горка для катания, 16	**gor**ka dlya kata**nee**ya	skiing
горные лыжи, 51	**gor**niye **li**zhee	slide
горох, 34	ga**roh**	peas
горячий, 44	ga**rya**chee	hot
гостиная, 4	ga**stee**naya	living room
гостиница, 12	ga**stee**neetsa	hotel
готовить еду, 43	ga**to**veet' ye**doo**	to cook
грабли, 9	**grab**lee	rake
гребля, 50	**gryeb**lya	rowing
грейпфрут, 34	greyp**froot**	grapefruit
гриб, 34	**greeb**	mushroom
грим, 15	**greem**	face paints

грудь, 38	**grood'**	chest
грузовик, 13	grooza**veek**	lorry
груша, 31	**groo**sha	pear
грязный, 44	**gryaz**niy	dirty
губка, 4	**goob**ka	sponge
губная гармошка, 14	goob**na**ya gar**mosh**ka	mouth organ
губы, 38	**goo**bi	lips
гусеница, 9	**goos**yeneetsa	caterpillar
гуси, 24	**goo**see	geese

Д

далеко, 44	dalye**ko**	far
два, 53	**dva**	two
двадцать, 53	**dva**tsat'	twelve
двенадцать, 53	dvye**nat**sat'	twenty
дверная ручка, 29	dvyer**na**ya **rooch**ka	door handle
дверь, 6	**dver'**	door
двигатель, 20	**dvee**gatyel'	(car) engine
двоюродный брат, 41	dva**yoo**radniy **brat**	cousin
девочка, 29	**dyev**achka	girl
девятнадцать, 53	dyevyat**nat**sat'	nineteen
девять, 53	**dyev**yat'	nine
Дед Мороз, 47	**dyed** ma**roz**	Father Christmas
дедушка, 41	**dyed**ooshka	grandfather
делать, 42	**dyel**at'	to make
дельтапланеризм, 51	dyel'ta-planye**reezm**	hang-gliding
дельфин, 18	dyel'**feen**	dolphin
день рождения, 47	**dyen'** razh**dyen**eeya	birthday
деньги, 35	**dyen'**gee	money
деревня, 23	de**ryev**nya	village
дерево, 9	**der**yeva	tree
деревья, 17	de**ryev'**ya	trees
десять, 53	**dyes**yat'	ten
дети, 17	**dyet**ee	children
джем, 36	**djem**	jam
джемпер, 39	**djem**pyer	jumper
джинсы, 39	**djeen**si	jeans
дзюдо, 51	dzyoo**do**	judo
диспетчерская вышка, 21	dees**pyetch**erskaya **vish**ka	control tower
длинный, 45	**dleen**niy	long
дни, 46	**dnee**	days
дождь, 48	**doshd'**	rain
дом, 13	**dom**	house, block of flats
дом на ферме, 25	**dom** na **fyer**mye	farmhouse
дома, 4	**do**ma	at home
домашние животные, 49	da**mash**neeye zhi**vot**niye	pets
дорога, 22	da**ro**ga	road
дорожный указатель, 22	da**rozh**niy ooka**za**tyel'	signpost
доска, 10	da**ska**	plank
доска, 28	da**ska**	board
дочь, 41	**doch'**	daughter
драться, 43	**drat'**sa	to fight
дрель, 10	**dryel'**	(hand) drill
дрессировщик, 55	dryessee-**rov**shcheek	ringmaster
дрова, 11	dra**va**	wood
думать, 42	**doo**mat'	to think
дуть, 43	**doot'**	to blow
душ, 4	**doosh**	shower
дым, 9	**dim**	smoke
дыня, 34	**din**ya	melon
дядя, 41	**dya**dya	uncle

е

еда, 36	ye**da**	food
есть, 42	**yest'**	to eat

ё

ёж, 22	**yozh**	hedgehog
ёлка, 47	**yol**ka	Christmas tree

Ж

жаба, 23	*zhaba*	toad
жалюзи, 29	*zhalyoozee*	(window) blind
ждать, 43	*zhdat'*	to wait
железная дорога, 14	*zhelyeznaya daroga*	train set
железная дорога, 20	*zhelyeznaya daroga*	railway track
жена, 41	*zhena*	wife
жених, 47	*zheneeh*	bridegroom
женщина, 13	*zhenshcheena*	woman
женщина-милиционер, 40	*zhenshcheena-meelee-tseeanyer*	policewoman
жёлтый, 52	*zholtiy*	yellow
живая изгородь, 9	*zhivaya eezgarad'*	hedge
живой, 45	*zhivoy*	alive
живот, 38	*zhivot*	tummy
жираф, 18	*zhiraf*	giraffe
жонглёр, 55	*zhanglyor*	juggler

З

забор, 17	*zabor*	railings
забор, 25	*zabor*	fence
завтрак, 36	*zavtrak*	breakfast
закрытый, 44	*zakritiy*	closed
залезать, 43	*zalyezat'*	to climb
замок, 14	*zamak*	castle
замок из песка, 26	*zamak eez pyeska*	sandcastle
занавеска, 30	*zana-vyeska*	curtain
занятия, 42	*zanyateeya*	doing things
звезда, 46, 52	*zvyezda*	star
зебра, 19	*zyebra*	zebra
зелёный, 52	*zyelyoniy*	green
земля, 17	*zyemlya*	earth
земля, 24	*zyemlya*	mud
зеркало, 5	*zyerkala*	mirror
зима, 48	*zeema*	winter
змея, 19	*zmeya*	snake
значок, 29	*znachok*	badge
золотая рыбка, 49	*zalataya ribka*	goldfish
зонтик, 26, 48	*zonteek*	umbrella
зоопарк, 18	*zaapark*	zoo
зубная паста, 4	*zoobnaya pasta*	toothpaste
зубная щётка, 4	*zoobnaya shchotka*	toothbrush
зубной врач, 41	*zoobnoy vrach*	dentist
зубы, 38	*zoobi*	teeth

И

игральные кости, 14	*eegral'niye kostee*	dice
играть, 43	*eegrat'*	to play
игрушки, 31, 32	*eegrooshkee*	toys
идти, 43	*eedtee*	to walk
индюки, 25	*eendyookee*	turkeys

Й

йогурт, 35	*yogoort*	yoghurt

К

какао, 36	*kakao*	hot chocolate
календарь, 10, 46	*kalyendar'*	calendar
калитка, 16	*kaleetka*	gate
камни, 22	*kamnee*	stones
камни, 23	*kamnee*	rocks
канал, 23	*kanal*	canal
канарейка, 49	*kanaryeyka*	canary
канат, 27	*kanat*	rope
канат, 55	*kanat*	tightrope
канатоходец, 55	*kanata-hodyets*	tightrope walker
капот, 21	*kapot*	(car) bonnet
капуста, 34	*kapoosta*	cabbage
карандаш, 28	*karandash*	pencil
карандаши, 29	*karandashee*	crayons
каратэ, 50	*karate*	karate

карманы, 39	*karmani*	pockets
карта, 29	*karta*	map
картинка-конструктор, 30	*karteenka-kanstrooktar*	jigsaw
картины, 5	*karteeni*	pictures
картофель, 35, 37	*kartofel'*	potatoes
картофельное пюре, 37	*kartofel'naye pyoore*	mashed potatoes
карусель, 54	*karoosyel'*	roundabout
касса, 35	*kassa*	checkout
касса-автомат, 20	*kassa-avtamat*	ticket machine
кассета, 33	*kassyeta*	cassette tape
кастрюли, 6	*kastryoolee*	saucepans
каток, 13, 15	*katok*	roller
кафе, 12	*ka-fe*	cafe
кафель, 7	*kafyel'*	tiles
качели, 16	*kachyelee*	swings
качели, 17	*kachyelee*	seesaw
квадрат, 52	*kvadrat*	square
кенгуру, 18	*kengooroo*	kangaroo
кепка, 39	*kyepka*	cap
кинотеатр, 13	*keenateatr*	cinema
кирпичи, 8	*keerpeechee*	bricks
кисточка, 29	*keestoshka*	paintbrush
кисть руки, 38	*keest' rookee*	hand
кит, 19	*keet*	whale
кладовка, 7	*kladovka*	cupboard
клей, 28	*kley*	glue
клетка, 49	*klyetka*	cage
клоун, 55	*klo-oon*	clown
клубника, 33	*kloobneeka*	strawberry
клумба, 17	*kloomba*	flower bed
клюв, 49	*klyoof*	beak
ключ, 6	*klyooch*	key
книги, 28	*kneegee*	books
кнопки, 11	*knopkee*	tacks
кнопки, 28	*knopkee*	drawing pins
ковёр, 4	*kavyor*	carpet
коврик, 5	*kovreek*	rug
коза, 19	*kaza*	goat
колготки, 39	*kalgotkee*	tights
колено, 38	*kalyena*	knee
колесо, 20	*kalyeso*	wheel
колесо обозрения, 54	*kalyeso aba-zryeneeya*	big wheel
колли, 24	*kollee*	sheepdog
кольцо, 14	*kal'tso*	ring
кольцо, 55	*kal'tso*	hoop
коляска, 9	*kalyaska*	pram
комиксы, 31	*komeeksi*	comic
комод, 5	*kamod*	chest of drawers
компакт-диск, 4	*kampakt deesk*	CD
компьютер, 31	*kamp'yooter*	computer
консервы, 35	*kansyervi*	tins
контролёр, 20	*kantralyor*	ticket inspector
конус, 52	*konoos*	cone
конфета, 32	*kanfyeta*	sweet
коньки, 51	*kan'kee*	ice skates
конюшня, 25	*kanyooshnya*	stable
копать, 42	*kapat'*	to dig
копилка, 15	*kapeelka*	money box
корабль, 27	*karabl'*	ship
корзина, 31, 35, 49	*karzeena*	basket
коричневый, 52	*kareechnyeviy*	brown
корм, 49	*korm*	petfood
коробка, 29	*karopka*	box
корова, 25	*karova*	cow
коровник, 25	*karovneek*	cowshed
короткий, 45	*karotkee*	short
космонавт, 40	*kasmanaft*	astronaut
космонавты, 15	*kasmanafti*	spacemen
космос, 46	*kosmas*	space
костёр, 9	*kastyor*	bonfire
костыли, 30	*kastilee*	crutches
кость, 9	*kost'*	bone

котёнок, 49	katyonak	kitten
кофе, 36	kofye	coffee
кофта, 39	kofta	cardigan
кошелёк, 35	kashelyok	purse
кошка, 49	koshka	cat
краб, 26	krab	crab
кран, 4	kran	tap
краски, 15, 28	kraskee	paints
красный, 52	krasniy	red
кресло-каталка, 30	kryesla-katalka	wheelchair
крикет, 50	kreekyet	cricket
кровать, 4	kravat'	bed
крокодил, 18	krakadeel	crocodile
кролик, 49, 55	kroleek	rabbit
кроссовки, 39	krassovkee	trainers
крот, 23	krot	mole
круг, 52	kroog	circle
крыло, 18	krilo	wing
крыша, 12	krisha	roof
куб, 52	koob	cube
кубики, 14	koobeekee	building blocks
куклы, 14	kookli	dolls
кукольный дом, 14	kookal'niy dom	doll's house
купальник, 27	koopal'neek	swimsuit
куртка, 39	koortka	jacket
куры, 25	koori	hens
курятник, 24	kooryatneek	henhouse
куст, 16	koost	bush
кухня, 6	koohnya	kitchen
кухонное полотенце, 7	koohannaye palatyentse	tea towel

Л

лампа, 5	lampa	lamp
лампочка, 33	lampachka	light bulb
лапы, 18	lapi	paws
ласты, 27	lasti	flippers
лебеди, 17	lyebedee	swans
лев, 18	lyev	lion
левый, 44	lyeviy	left
легко, 45	lyehko	easy
лейка, 8	leyka	watering can
лекарство, 30	lyekarstva	medicine
лента, 32	lyenta	ribbon
леопард, 19	lyeapard	leopard
лес, 22	lyes	forest
лестница, 5	lestneetsa	stairs
лестница, 9, 10	lestneetsa	ladder
лестница, 13	lestneetsa	steps
лето, 48	lyeta	summer
летучая мышь, 18	lyetoochaya mish'	bat (animal)
лимон, 34	leemon	lemon
линейка, 28	leenyeyka	ruler
лиса, 22	leesa	fox
листья, 9	leest'ya	leaves
лисята, 23	leesyata	fox cubs
лифт, 30	leeft	lift
лицо, 38	leetso	face
ловить, 42	laveet'	to catch
ложки, 7	lozhkee	spoons
локомотив, 20	lakamateev	(train) engine
локоть, 38	lokat'	elbow
ломать, 42	lamat'	to break
лопата, 8, 26	lapata	spade
лошадь, 25, 51	loshad'	horse
лошадь-качалка, 15	loshad'-kachalka	rocking horse
лужа, 17	loozha	puddle
лук, 15	look	bow
лук, 34	look	onion
лук-порей, 34	look-parey	leek
луна, 46	loona	moon
луна-парк, 54	loona-park	fairground
лыжи, 51	lizhee	ski
лыжная палка, 51	lizhnaya palka	ski pole

львята, 18	l'vyata	lion cubs
люди, 40	lyoodee	people
лягушка, 16	lyagooshka	frog

M

магазин, 12, 34	magazeen	shop
магазин игрушек, 14	magazeen eegrooshek	toyshop
майка, 39	mayka	vest
маленький, 44	malyen'kee	small
малина, 33	maleena	raspberry
мало, 44	mala	few
малыш, 17	malish	baby
мальчик, 28	mal'cheek	boy
маляр, 41	malyar	painter
мандарин, 33	mandareen	clementine
марионетки, 15	mareea-nyetkee	puppets
маскарадные костюмы, 33	maska-radniye kastyoomi	fancy dress
маски, 15	maskee	masks
масло, 21	masla	oil
масло, 33	masla	butter
мастерская, 10	mastyerskaya	workshop
мат, 54	mat	mat
мать, 41	mat'	mother
машина, 13	masheena	car
машинист, 20	masheeneest	train driver
маяк, 26	mayak	lighthouse
медбрат, 30	myedbrat	(male) nurse
медведь, 18	myedvyed'	bear
медленно, 45	myedlyenna	slow
мел, 28	myel	chalk
механики, 40	myehaneekee	mechanics
мёд, 36	myod	honey
мёртвый, 45	myortviy	dead
милицейская машина, 12	meelee-tseyskaya masheena	police car
милиционер, 13, 40	meelee-tseeanyer	policeman
миски, 7	meeskee	bowls
мишень, 51	meeshyen'	target
много, 44	mnoga	many
мойка, 6	moyka	sink
мокрый, 44	mokriy	wet
молния, 39	molneeya	zip
молния, 48	molneeya	lightning
молоко, 36, 49	malako	milk
молоток, 11	malatok	hammer
мольберт, 29	mal'byert	easel
море, 26	morye	sea
морковь, 34	markov'	carrot
мороженое, 16	marozhenaye	ice cream
мороз, 48	maroz	frost
морская звезда, 26	marskaya zvyezda	starfish
морская свинка, 49	marskaya sveenka	guinea pig
моряк, 26	maryak	sailor
мост, 23	most	bridge
моторка, 26	matorka	motor-boat
мотоцикл, 13	matatseekl	motorcycle
мотыга, 8	matiga	hoe
мотылёк, 23	matilyok	moth
моя, 39	maya	my
муж, 41	moozh	husband
мужчина, 12	moozhcheena	man
мука, 35	mooka	flour
мусор, 6	moosar	rubbish
мусорное ведро, 29	moosarnaye vyedro	wastepaper bin
мусорный бак, 8	moosarniy bak	dustbin
муха, 11	mooha	fly
мыло, 4	mila	soap
мыть, 42	mit'	to wash
мышь, 49	mish'	mouse
мягкий, 45	myahkee	soft
мясник, 40	myasneek	butcher
мясо, 35	myasa	meat
мяч, 17, 50	myach	ball

Н

набрось-кольцо, 54	na**bros'**-kal'**tso**	hoop-la
наверху, 45	na**vyerhoo**	upstairs
над, 44	**nad**	over
наездница, 55	na**yez**neetsa	bareback rider
наждачная бумага, 10	nazh**dach**naya boo**ma**ga	sandpaper
наживка, 50	na**zhiv**ka	bait
напильник, 11	na**peel'**neek	file
настольная лампа, 29	na**stol'**naya **lam**pa	desk lamp
настольный теннис, 51	na**stol'**niy **ten**nees	table tennis
небо, 48	**nyeb**a	sky
невеста, 47	nye**vyes**ta	bride
нести, 42	nye**stee**	to carry
нижний, 44	**neezh**nee	bottom (not top)
низко, 45	**neez**ka	low
новый, 45	**no**viy	new
нога, 38	na**ga**	leg
ножи, 7	na**zhee**	knives
ножницы, 28	**nozh**neetsi	scissors
нос, 38	**nos**	nose
носки, 39	nas**kee**	socks
носовой платок, 39	nasa**voy** pla**tok**	handkerchief
носорог, 19	nasa**rog**	rhinoceros
ночная рубашка, 31	nach**na**ya roo**bash**ka	nightdress
ночь, 46	**noch'**	night

О

обед, 36	a**byed**	lunch
обезьяна, 18	abyez'**ya**na	monkey
облака, 48	**ob**laka	clouds
овал, 52	a**val**	oval
овощи, 34	**o**vashchee	vegetables
овцы, 25	**ov**tsi	sheep
огурец, 34	agoo**ryets**	cucumber
одежда, 39	a**dyezh**da	clothes
один, 53	a**deen**	one
одиннадцать, 53	a**deen**natsat'	eleven
ожерелье, 14	azher**yel'**ye	necklace
озеро, 16	**o**zyera	lake
окно, 32	ak**no**	window
олень, 19	a**len'**	deer
омлет, 37	am**lyet**	omelette
опилки, 10	a**peel**kee	sawdust
оранжевый, 52	a**ran**jeviy	orange (colour)
орёл, 18	ar**yol**	eagle
оркестр, 55	ar**kyes**tr	band
оса, 8	a**sa**	wasp
осень, 48	**o**syen'	autumn
ослик, 27	**o**sleek	donkey
остров, 26	**o**strav	island
отбойный молоток, 12	at**boy**niy mala**tok**	(pneumatic) drill
отвёртка, 10	at**vyort**ka	screwdriver
отец, 41	a**tyets**	father
открытки, 31	at**krit**kee	cards
открытый, 44	at**kri**tiy	open
отпуск, 47	**ot**poosk	holiday
официант, 41	afee-tsee**ant**	waiter
официантка, 41	afee-tsee**ant**ka	waitress

П

падать, 43	**pa**dat'	to fall
пакет, 34	pa**kyet**	carrier bag
палатки, 23	pa**lat**kee	tents
палка, 31	**pal**ka	walking stick
палочки, 37	pa**lach**kee	chopsticks
пальто, 39	pal'**to**	coat
пальцы, 38	**pal'**tsi	fingers
пальцы ноги, 38	**pal'**tsi na**gee**	toes
панда, 18	**pan**da	panda
парашют, 15	para**shoot**	parachute
парикмахер, 41	pareek-**ma**hyer	hairdresser
парк, 16	**park**	park
парусник, 26	**pa**roosneek	sailing boat
парусный спорт, 50	**pa**roosniy **sport**	sailing
пастушка, 25	pa**stoosh**ka	shepherdess
паук, 11	**pa**-ook	spider
паутина, 11	pa-oo**tee**na	cobweb
певцы, 40	pyev**tsi**	singers
пекарь, 41	**pyek**ar'	baker
пеликан, 18	pelee**kan**	pelican
первый, 44	**pyer**viy	first
переход, 13	pere**hod**	crossing
перец, 36	**pyer**yets	pepper
перочинный нож, 10	pyera**cheen**niy **nozh**	penknife
персик, 34	**pyer**seek	peach
перчатки, 39	pyer**chat**kee	gloves
перья, 18	**pyer'**ya	feathers
песочница, 16	pe**soch**neetsa	sandpit
петли, 39	**pyet**lee	button holes
петух, 24	pye**tooh**	cockerel
петь, 43	**pyet'**	to sing
печенье, 33	pye**chen'**ye	biscuit
пижама, 31	pee**zha**ma	pyjamas
пикник, 16	peek**neek**	picnic
пила, 10	pee**la**	saw
пилот, 21	pee**lot**	pilot
пингвин, 18	peeng**veen**	penguin
писать, 42	pee**sat'**	to write
письма, 5	**pees'**ma	letters
письменный стол, 28	**pees'**myenniy **stol**	desk
пить, 42	**peet'**	to drink
пицца, 37	**peet**sa	pizza
плавание, 50	**pla**vaneeye	swimming
плакать, 42	**pla**kat'	to cry
планета, 46	pla**nyet**a	planet
пластилин, 15	plastee**leen**	modelling clay
пластырь, 31	**plas**tir'	sticking plaster
платформа, 20	plat**for**ma	platform
платье, 39	**plat'**ye	dress
плечи, 38	**plyech**ee	shoulders
плита, 7	plee**ta**	cooker
плотник, 40	**plot**neek	carpenter
плохой, 44	pla**hoy**	bad
площадка для игр, 12	plash**chad**ka dlya **eegr**	playground
плуг, 25	**ploog**	plough
плюшевый мишка, 30	**plyoo**sheviy **meesh**ka	teddy bear
пляж, 27	**plyazh**	beach
повар, 40	**po**var	chef
поводок, 17	pava**dok**	dog lead
погода, 48	pa**go**da	weather
под, 44	**pod**	under
подарок, 47	pa**da**rak	present
подарки, 32	pa**dar**kee	presents
подбородок, 38	padba**ro**dak	chin
подводная лодка, 14	pad**vod**naya **lod**ka	submarine
подгузник, 31	pad**goos**neek	nappy
подметать, 43	padmye**tat'**	to sweep
поднос, 30	pad**nos**	tray
подружка невесты, 47	pa**droosh**ka nye**vyes**ti	bridesmaid
подушка, 4	pa**doosh**ka	cushion
подушка, 5	pa**doosh**ka	pillow
подъёмник, 51	pa**dyom**neek	chairlift
подъёмный кран, 15	pa**dyom**niy **kran**	crane
поезд, 23	**po**yest	train
поезд с привидениями, 54	**po**yest spreevee-**dyen**eeyamee	ghost train
пожарная машина, 13	pa**zhar**naya ma**shee**na	fire engine
пожарник, 40	pa**zhar**neek	fireman
поздравительная открытка, 47	pazdra-**vee**tel'naya at**krit**ka	birthday card
покупать, 43	pakoo**pat'**	to buy

пол, 29	**pol**	floor
поле, 25	**pol**ye	field
ползти, 42	pal**stee**	to crawl
поливальная установка, 8	palee-**val'**naya oosta**nov**ka	sprinkler
полный, 45	**pol**niy	full
полотенце, 4	pala**tyen**tse	towel
полумесяц, 52	paloo-**myes**yats	crescent
помидор, 34	pamee**dor**	tomato
понедельник, 46	panye**dyel'**neek	Monday
пони, 51	**po**nee	pony
попкорн, 54	pap**korn**	popcorn
попугай, 49	papoo**gay**	parrot
поросята, 25	para**sya**ta	piglets
последний, 44	pa**slyed**nee	last
потолок, 29	pata**lok**	ceiling
почтальон, 41	pachtal'**on**	postman
правый, 45	**pra**viy	right
праздники, 47	**praz**neekee	special days
праздничный торт, 47	**praz**neechniy **tort**	birthday cake
приёмная, 31	pree**yom**naya	waiting room
примеры, 28	pree**myer**i	sums
прицеп, 13	pree**tsep**	trailer
прогулочная коляска, 17	pra**goo**-lachnaya ka**lyas**ka	pushchair
простыня, 5	prasti**nya**	sheet
пруд, 24	**prood**	pond
прыгать, 42	**pri**gat'	to skip
прыгать, 43	**pri**gat'	to jump
прыжки в воду, 50	prish**kee vvo**doo	diving
пряжка, 39	**pryash**ka	buckle
прямоугольник, 52	pryama-oo**gol'**neek	rectangle
прятаться, 43	**prya**tat'sa	to hide
птицы, 17	**ptee**tsi	birds
пугало, 25	**poo**gala	scarecrow
пуговицы, 39	**poo**gaveetsi	buttons
пудинг, 37	**poo**deeng	pudding
пурпурный, 52	poor**poor**niy	purple
пустой, 45	poo**stoy**	empty
путешествие, 20	pootye-**shest**veeye	travel
пуховое одеяло, 5	poo**ho**vaye adye**ya**la	duvet
пчела, 9	pchye**la**	bee
пылесос, 6	pilye**sos**	vacuum cleaner
пятнадцать, 53	pyat**nat**sat'	fifteen
пятница, 46	**pyat**neetsa	Friday
пять, 53	**pyat'**	five

р

радио, 4	**ra**deeo	radio
радуга, 48	**ra**dooga	rainbow
разговаривать, 42	razga-**va**reevat'	to talk
раздевалка, 51	razdye-**val**ka	changing room
ракета, 15	ra**kyet**a	rocket
ракета, 46	ra**kyet**a	spaceship
ракетка, 50	ra**kyet**ka	racket
раковина, 4	**ra**kaveena	washbasin
раковина, 26	**ra**kaveena	shell
растение, 29	ra**styen**eeye	plant
расчёска, 5	ra**schos**ka	comb
регби, 50	**reg**bee	rugby
резать, 42	**ryez**at'	to cut
резинка, 28	rye**zeen**ka	rubber
река, 22	rye**ka**	river
ремень, 39	rye**men'**	belt
рис, 37	**rees**	rice
рисовать, 42	reesa**vat'**	to paint
рисунок, 28	ree**soo**nak	drawing
робот, 14	**ro**bat	robot
рога, 19	ra**ga**	horns
Рождество, 47	razhdest**vo**	Christmas day
розовый, 52	**ro**zaviy	pink
ролики, 16	**ro**leekee	roller blades
ромб, 52	**romb**	diamond
роса, 48	ra**sa**	dew

рот, 38	**rot**	mouth
рояль, 15	ra**yal'**	piano
рубанок, 11	roo**ba**nak	shaving plane
рубашка, 39	roo**bash**ka	shirt
рубить, 42	roo**beet'**	to chop
ружьё, 15	roozh'**yo**	gun
рука, 38	roo**ka**	arm
рулетка, 11	roo**lyet**ka	tape measure
ручей, 22	roo**chey**	stream
ручка, 28	**rooch**ka	pen
рыба, 27	**ri**ba	fish
рыбак, 23	ri**bak**	fisherman
рыбалка, 50	ri**bal**ka	fishing
рыбачья лодка, 27	ri**bach'**ya **lod**ka	fishing boat
рынок, 13	**ri**nak	market
рюкзак, 20	ryook**zak**	backpack

с

сад, 8	**sad**	garden
сад, 25	**sad**	orchard
салат, 34	sa**lat**	lettuce
салат, 37	sa**lat**	salad
салфетки, 31	sal**fyet**kee	tissues
салями, 33	sa**lya**mee	salami
самолёт, 21	sama**lyot**	plane
сандали, 39	san**da**lee	sandals
сани, 47	**sa**nee	sleigh
сапоги, 39	sapa**gee**	boots
сарай, 8	sa**ray**	shed
сахар, 36	**sa**har	sugar
сахарная вата, 54	**sa**harnaya **va**ta	candy floss
свадьба, 47	**svad'**ba	wedding day
светло, 45	svyet**lo**	light
светофор, 13	svyeta**for**	traffic lights
свеча, 32, 47	svye**cha**	candle
свинарник, 24	svee**nar**neek	pigsty
свиньи, 25	**sveen'**ee	pigs
свисток, 14	svee**stok**	whistle
свитер, 39	**svee**ter	sweatshirt
северный олень, 47	**sye**verniy a**len'**	reindeer
седло, 25	syed**lo**	saddle
сельдерей, 34	syel'**de**rey	celery
сельская местность, 22	**syel'**skaya **myest**nast'	country
семафор, 20	sema**for**	signals
семена, 8	syeme**na**	seeds
семнадцать, 53	syem**nat**sat'	seventeen
семь, 53	**syem'**	seven
семья, 41	syem'**ya**	families
сено, 25	**sye**na	hay
серый, 52	**sye**riy	grey
сестра, 41	syes**tra**	sister
сеть, 27	**syet'**	net
сзади, 45	sza**dee**	behind
сидеть, 43	see**dyet'**	to sit
синий, 52	**see**nee	blue
скакалка, 17	ska**kal**ka	skipping rope
скамейка, 16	ska**myey**ka	bench
скатерть, 33	**ska**tyert'	tablecloth
скейтборд, 17	**skeyt**bord	skateboard
сковорода, 7	skavara**da**	frying pan
скорая помощь, 12	**sko**raya **po**mashch'	ambulance
слива, 35	**slee**va	plum
сливки, 36	**sleev**kee	cream
слон, 19	**slon**	elephant
слушать, 42	**sloo**shat'	to listen
смеяться, 42	sme**yat'**sa	to laugh
смотреть, 43	sma**tryet'**	to watch
снаружи, 45	sna**roo**zhee	out
снег, 48	**snyeg**	snow
сноубординг, 50	sno-oo**bor**deeng	snowboarding
собака, 16, 49, 55	sa**ba**ka	dog
собирать, 43	sabee**rat'**	to pick
сова, 23	**sa**va	owl

61

совок, 7	sa**vok**	dustpan
совок, 9	sa**vok**	trowel
солдатики, 15	sal**da**teekee	soldiers
солнце, 46, 48	**soln**tse	sun
соломинка, 32	sa**lo**meenka	straw
соль, 36	**sol**'	salt
сосиска, 33	sa**sees**ka	sausage
соус, 37	**so**-oos	sauce
софа, 4	sa**fa**	sofa
спагетти, 37	spa**get**tee	spaghetti
спальня, 5	**spal**'nya	bedroom
спать, 43	**spat**'	to sleep
спереди, 45	**sper**yedee	in front
спина, 38	spee**na**	back (of body)
спички, 7	**speech**kee	matches
спорт, 50	**sport**	sport
среда, 46	sry**eda**	Wednesday
стаканы, 6	sta**ka**ni	glasses (for drinking)
старый, 45	**sta**riy	old
стена, 29	sty**ena**	wall
стиральная машина, 7	stee**ral**'naya ma**shee**na	washing mashine
стиральный порошок, 6	stee**ral**'niy para**shok**	washing powder
стог, 24	**stok**	haystack
стол, 5	**stol**	table
страус, 18	**stra**oos	ostrich
стрелы, 14	**stry**eli	arrows
стрельба из лука, 51	stryel'**ba** eez **loo**ka	archery
стружки, 10	**stroosh**kee	shavings
стул, 5	**stool**	chair
ступня, 38	stoop**nya**	foot
стюард, 21	styoo**ard**	air steward
стюардесса, 21	styooar**des**sa	air hostess
суббота, 46	soob**bo**ta	Saturday
судья, 40	sood'**ya**	judge
сумочка, 35	**soo**machka	handbag
суп, 37	**soop**	soup
сухой, 44	soo**hoy**	dry
сын, 41	**sin**	son
сыр, 33, 34	**seer**	cheese

Т

таблетки, 30	ta**blyet**kee	pills
табурет, 6	taboo**ryet**	stool
такси, 13	tak**see**	taxi
танкер, 27	**tan**kyer	oil tanker (ship)
танцевать, 42	tantse**vat**'	to dance
танцоры, 40	tan**tso**ri	dancers
танцы, 50	**tan**tsi	dance
тарелки, 7	ta**ryel**kee	plates
тачка, 8	**tach**ka	wheelbarrow
твёрдый, 45	**tvyor**diy	hard
телевизор, 31	tele**vee**zar	television
тележка, 24	tye**lyesh**ka	cart
тележка, 35	tye**lyesh**ka	trolley
телескоп, 46	tyele**skop**	telescope
телефон, 5	tele**fon**	telephone
телёнок, 25	tye**lyo**nak	calf
темно, 45	tyem**no**	dark
теннис, 50	**ten**nees	tennis
теплица, 9	tye**pleet**sa	greenhouse
термометр, 30	tyer**mo**metr	thermometer
тетрадь, 29	tye**trad**'	notebook
тётя, 41	**tyo**tya	aunt
тигр, 19	**tee**gr	tiger
тир, 54	**teer**	rifle range
тиски, 10	tee**skee**	vice
товарный поезд, 20	ta**var**niy **po**yest	goods train
толкать, 43	tal**kat**'	to push
толстый, 44	**tol**stiy	fat
тонкий, 44	**ton**kee	thin
топор, 11	ta**por**	axe
торт, 32	**tort**	cake

тосты, 36	**tos**ti	toast
трава, 9	tra**va**	grass
трактор, 24	**trak**tar	tractor
трапеция, 55	tra**pyet**seeya	trapeze
треугольник, 52	trye-oo**gol**'neek	triangle
трёхколесный велосипед, 17	tryohkal-**yos**niy vyela-see**pyed**	tricycle
три, 53	**tree**	three
тринадцать, 53	tree**nat**sat'	thirteen
тропинка, 9, 16	tra**peen**ka	path
тротуар, 12	trato**oar**	pavement
труба, 12	troo**ba**	chimney
труба, 14	troo**ba**	trumpet
трубы, 12	**troo**bi	pipes
трудно, 45	**trood**na	difficult
трусы, 39	**troo**see	pants
тряпка для пыли, 7	**tryap**ka dlya **pi**lee	duster
туалетная бумага, 4	tooa**lyet**-naya boo**ma**ga	toilet paper
туман, 48	too**man**	fog, mist
туннель, 23	too**nel**'	tunnel
тыква, 35	**tik**va	pumpkin
тюлень, 19	tyoo**len**'	seal
тянуть, 43	tya**noot**'	to pull

У

у моря, 26	oo **mo**rya	seaside
удочка, 50	**oo**dachka	fishing rod
ужин, 37	**oo**zheen	dinner, supper
улей, 8	**oo**ley	beehive
улитка, 8	oo**leet**ka	snail
улица, 12	**oo**leetsa	street
уличный фонарь, 13	**oo**leechniy fa**nar**'	lamp post
улыбаться, 42	ooli**bat**'sa	to smile
унитаз, 4	oonee**taz**	toilet
утёс, 27	oo**tyos**	cliff
утки, 17, 24	**oot**kee	ducklings
утро, 46	**oo**tra	morning
утюг, 7	oo**tyoog**	iron
утята, 17, 24	oo**tya**ta	ducks
учительница, 29	oo**chee**tel'neetsa	teacher
уши, 38	**oo**shee	ears

Ф

фабрика, 13	**fab**reeka	factory
фартук, 6	**far**took	apron
фары, 20	**fa**ri	headlights
фейерверк, 32	feyer**vyerk**	fireworks
ферма, 24	**fyer**ma	farm
фермер, 25	**fyer**myer	farmer
фигурное катание, 51	fee**goor**naye ka**ta**neeye	ice-skating
фигуры, 52	fee**goo**ri	shapes
физкультура, 50	feeskool'-**too**ra	exercise
флаг, 26	**flag**	flag
фломастеры, 28	fla**mas**teri	felt-tips
фотоаппарат, 14, 47	fota-appa**rat**	camera
фотограф, 47	fa**to**graf	photographer
фотографии, 28	fata**gra**fee	photographs
фруктовый сок, 33	frook**to**viy **sok**	fruit juice
фрукты, 34	**frook**ti	fruit
фургон, 13	foor**gon**	van
футбол, 51	foot**bol**	football
футболка, 39	foot**bol**ka	T-shirt

Х

халат, 30	ha**lat**	dressing gown
хвост, 18	**hvost**	tail
хлеб, 33	**hlyeb**	bread
хлопья, 36	**hlop**'ya	cereal
хобот, 19	**ho**bat	trunk
холл, 5	**holl**	hall

Designed by Andy Griffin
Cover design by Hannah Ahmed

This revised edition first published in 2005 by Usborne Publishing Ltd., Usborne House, 83-85 Saffron Hill, London EC1N 8RT, England. www.usborne.com